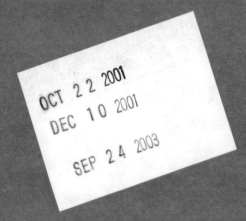

Corvette

AMERICA'S SUPERCAR

BY JOHN LAMM

CHARTWELL
BOOKS, INC.

A QUINTET BOOK

ISBN 0-7858-0341-6

This book was designed and produced by
Quintet Publishing Limited
6, Blundell Street
London N7 9BH

Creative Director: Peter Bridgewater
Art Director: Ian Hunt
Designer: Annie Moss
Editor: Shaun Barrington
Jacket Design: Nik Morley

Typeset in Great Britain by
Central Southern Typesetters, Eastbourne
Manufactured in China by
Regent Publishing Services Ltd.

Published by Chartwell Books
A Division of Book Sales, Inc.
P.O. Box 7100
Edison, New Jersey 08818–7100

CONTENTS

INTRODUCTION

SETTING THE STAGE

MONTEREY 1987:
*Harlow Curtice's own
custom '56 leads a parade
of venerable Corvette
specials.*

Every hard figure GM had in the early '50s made the Corvette look like a bad idea. That's not to say it was a bad car – far from it. But the chances of making a profit with a 2-seat, European-style sports car were slim indeed, and the General must have known it.

America's sports car market was limited to a very small, very elite group of buyers. Chevrolet sold two million units in 1950, while sports car builders as a whole managed to move perhaps 5000 vehicles across America.

But sports cars *seemed* hot. Magazines were filled with them. The suavest, smoothest servicemen had brought sleek coupes and roadsters back from the war and still turned heads with them. All the right people seemed to be interested – but interested and willing to buy are two very different things, a fact that's rarely lost on GM.

So the question is, *why*? Why in 1953 did General Motors tool up for, let alone expect to sell, 10,000 or more Corvettes in a matter of a few years?

Officially, the company had a simple explanation: They held that the reason sports cars had sold so poorly in America thus far had been because the only ones available were European cars built by Europeans for European conditions. A sports car tailored to the better roads, wider spaces, and traditions of comfort and luxury of the American market would sell to a much broader base.

In other words, General Motors was saying that the motorist who'd buy this car didn't even know he wanted it yet. How could he? It didn't *exist* yet. GM hoped to build a car and then create a market for it. Needless to say, that's not how it's usually done.

In reality, the decision to build the Corvette wasn't a simple profit/loss equation at all. GM knew full well the benefits that could come from a dignified failure. If the Corvette could do something toward changing Chevrolet's dowdy image, then it would be worth a little time and capital to let that happen. Should it run aground in the marketplace, the car could be quietly retired. And, to be honest, GM's decision to market the Corvette was also based a lot on wishful thinking. The movers and shakers of the company were serious car lovers, and they *wanted that car!* If they could bring such a beautiful machine to market, well, that in itself would be a triumph. They wanted to believe that there were car lovers just like themselves all across the country – ones who just hadn't

been tapped.

Had Chevy's sports car been allowed to die when the lack of public interest seemed to demand it around 1955, it would be remembered very differently today. It would have been a quick, classy, good-looking, and ill-fated image car: a sign of life from Detroit that was quashed before maturity.

There would have been no '55 V-8. No '57 Fuelie. No SS, Sting Ray, Grand Sport, Greenwood, or GTP. We'd have no RPO 684, no L88, no ZR1, *nothing*. Just a few years' worth of fascinating footnotes to the

ABOVE *The first 25 or so production cars came with domed wheelcovers. Unique Corvette spinners weren't ready yet.*

BELOW *Bob McLean placed the Blue Flame engine far back in the frame for a true sports car layout.*

history of America's oversized autos.

Of course that – to the great relief of the world's enthusiasts – isn't quite how it turned out. The irony of the Corvette story is that its main characters – men like Harley Earl, Ed Cole, Zora Arkus-Duntov, and the many, many others who've championed the Corvette for more than 35 years now – were 100% right. They had hoped and wished and felt in their guts that an American-style sports car would find an audience, and it did. There really *was* an untapped sports car market out there.

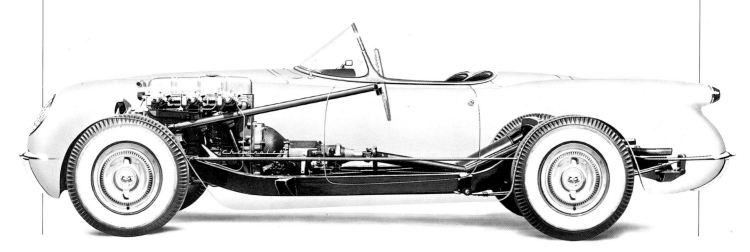

INTO

ITS

OWN

The chrome teeth of a '59.

1956 marked the first major body change since the Motorama Corvette's debut in 1953. It also marked the introduction of a much improved car.

Even though it had been quite successful in 1955, the 265-cid Turbo-Fire V-8 boasted a long list of improvements. Compression was bumped from 8.0 to 9.25:1. A new intake manifold carried a single Carter 4-barrel, giving 210 bhp @ 5200 rpm. An optional setup using two 4-barrels gave 225 bhp and 270 lb/ft of torque. Finned aluminum rocker covers now made the optional 225-horse engine look as special as it was, and ignition shielding was improved to prevent radio interference. An oil filter was added (1955's engine had overlooked that). A dual-point distributor was adopted to give stronger sparks to the uprated engine.

ZORA ARKUS-DUNTOV

Perhaps even more important to enthusiasts than the refinements to the V-8 was the widespread availability of the 3-speed manual transmission. This gearbox, now standard rather than optional, proved to be a delight despite its non-synchro first gear. A choice of rear-axle ratios – 3.70:1 standard and 4.11:1 or 3.27:1 optional on manual cars – tailored cruising and acceleration abilities to the needs of the individual driver.

Also much improved for '56 was the car's high-speed handling. A Belgian-born engineer named Zora Arkus-Duntov had come aboard to work on the 'Vette in 1953. After taking care of some of the car's more minor details, Duntov had turned his attention to that area.

Realizing that the front end was oversteering while its rear end understeered, Zora was surprised the Corvette behaved even as well as it did. He quickly shimmed up the suspension in key spots, altered the rear spring hangers, and generally got things set up correctly. Duntov, forever fiddling with the car's internals, would soon become the central figure of the Corvette program.

In the interior, too, the Corvette was thoroughly improved. Gone were the drafty side curtains. The car now sported roll-up windows with optional power lifts. Outside door locks and handles were specified to replace the previous car's interior-only handles. The folding top was improved mechanically and visually, and an optional power system raised

and lowered it automatically. For those wishing to forget the soft top altogether, Chevrolet offered an optional fiberglass hardtop. (The hardtop and roll-up windows first appeared on an otherwise stock Corvette in the 1954 Motorama.) Further interior improvements were a dealer-installed seatbelt package and a factory fresh-air heater.

Outside, the 1956 Corvette received a thorough workover. Its headlights muscled ahead into the airflow and the tail lights became faired in, giving an aggressive, crouching stance to the rear end. Two powerful-looking bulges flowed down the hood mimicking the Mercedes 300SL, which was sometimes also credited as the inspiration for the forward-swept headlights.

Also new for 1956 were the scalloped coves behind the Corvette's front wheels. These depressions would become a Corvette hallmark for the next seven years. Their true roots are murky, however, and somewhat in dispute.

Officially, Chevrolet took this cue from the 1955 LaSalle II and Biscayne dreamcars, both of which featured scooped-out sides of one form or another. In truth, the scoop-sided look must have come from myriad sources: Frank Kurtis' 500M and some Italian designs were already exploring it in the early '50s.

The '56 Corvette, however, was the first – perhaps the only – car to really get the shape *right*. While the concave scoops looked tacked on on most of the cars that got them, the Corvette's were so well done they could be highlighted with a chrome strip and contrasting colors.

What Chevrolet now had was simply one of the best sports cars in the world. It had a gorgeous new body, much-improved handling, considerable creature comforts, and one of the most potent yet tractable powertrains available at any cost. All that remained was to get the word out to the masses, and in this endeavor Chevrolet had enthusiastic help.

ABOVE LEFT *Often called the Father of the Corvette, Zora Arkus-Duntov could more accurately be called a protective guardian.*

TOP *Great-looking 1956 redesign and V-8 power got buyers back in line.*

ABOVE *John Fitch (pictured), Zora Arkus-Duntov, and Betty Skelton were Chevy's designated speed pilots at Daytona Beach, 1956.*

THE 1963-1967 STING RAY

FAITHFUL *to Mitchell's racer, the production Sting Ray was sleek, quick and less ornamented than previous Corvettes.*

Even though the popular and advanced '57 Corvette had just begun filling showrooms, Chevrolet engineers were already working on a replacement for 1960. Two years earlier they'd put considerable effort into an all-new Corvette for 1958, but that program was cancelled as unnecessarily expensive. The Q-Corvette, their project targeted for 1960, fell to a similar fate in the winter of 1957–1958.

A SMOOTHER RIDE

It wasn't until fall of 1959 that serious work began on a second-generation Corvette that would actually see production. And noting the Corvette's steadily rising sales from 1956 to 1962, it seems that GM was correct, at least in a business sense, in carrying the first generation on as long as it did.

Regardless, by late 1959 the body of the XP-720 – the car that would become the '63 'Vette – was taking shape along roughly the same lines as the Q-Corvette before it. Mechanically it was much simpler, retaining the body-on-frame construction, GRP skins, and front-mounted engine and transmission of the previous model. All these had been in question on the Q-Car, but they were definite for the XP-720.

While the layout was similar, the '63 would be a completely different car. The only components carried over would be the engine and transmission. The frame was a ladder design with boxed side rails and five crossmembers, rather than the old car's X-braced structure. The completely restyled body sat down in, not on, the new frame. The powerplant was offset one inch from the center (crowding the passenger's side) for increased driver legroom, better one-up balance, and proper driveshaft alignment over the offset rear-axle pinion.

The axle itself was independent, unlike the old car's. To achieve the handling, ride, and stability he wanted for the next-generation Corvette, Zora Arkus-Duntov had eagerly awaited the Q-Car's independent rear suspension. When the Q evaporated, Zora wasn't willing to let the frame-mounted rear end go with it.

IRS, or independent rear suspension, offers some distinct advantages over conventional live rear axles. The most obvious boon is that road irregularities and tire attitudes affecting one rear wheel aren't transferred immediately to the other, allowing both ride and handling to be greatly improved. But equally

The fixed-roof coupe originally outsold open cars by a healthy margin. Convertibles caught up toward the end of the year.

important is the reduction in unsprung weight IRS allows.

Sprung weight is the weight of the car that's isolated from the wheel assemblies by springs, shocks, and so on. Unsprung weight, of course, is just the opposite – the weight of the tires, wheels, brakes, and associated hardware that moves up and down in direct contact with the road.

The greater the ratio of sprung to unsprung weight, the smoother a car's ride. With a live rear axle, the entire differential and axle assembly counts as unsprung weight. With IRS, the differential is mounted to the frame and its weight is sprung, rather than unsprung. IRS helped drop the Corvette's unsprung weight by 33%, and the improvement in ride quality was immediately apparent.

GM engineers under Duntov's direction designed an unusual but very effective rear suspension, using U-jointed halfshafts as the upper locating links for the rear wheels. Struts below the shafts located the hubs' bottom end, while box-shaped trailing arms controlled fore-and-aft movement. Most controversial in design was the method of springing chosen: a single transverse leaf spring assembly – used on Henry Ford's Model T – acted on both wheels,

LEFT *The creased beltline and smooth deck of 1963 Corvettes was already familiar from the 1961 and 1962 models.*

BOTTOM *The famous split window: Duntov hated it, Mitchell loved it, and GM cancelled it after one year of production.*

Despite its age, the transverse spring turned out to be surprisingly efficient. (The current Corvette, possibly the best handling car in the world, uses it front and rear today.) The transverse spring was inexpensive, compact, and quite simply the best of the many options Chevrolet looked into.

The new ladder frame was no lighter than before, but it was stronger and less flexible. It was also shaped to allow the car's center of gravity to be lowered and overall height reduced 2.8 inches.

The frame's surprising heft was in part the result of a decision made while the new Corvette was still in its fetal stages. As Chevrolet's general manager, Ed

Cole realized that the Corvette would appeal to a broader market if it were a nominal 4-seater, rather than a 2-seater only. He ordered a 4-place prototype made to that end.

Mitchell, Duntov, and even most of the Chevrolet sales staff were against the idea, but GM Styling and Engineering reluctantly cobbled together a stretched 2+2 version of the XP-720. It was a gawky – perhaps intentionally so – effort, and Cole eventually gave in. Extra beef had been designed into the frame just in case the stretch went through, however, and that strength remained. Some stylists also point to the '63's rather upright windshield rake as a result of the 2+2 program.

Though interior and luggage space was actually better than that of the '62 model, the new car's wheelbase shrank from 102 to 98 inches. Between the tightened dimensions and an engine set farther back in the frame, the new Corvette's weight distribution became a near-perfect 49% front/51% rear split.

Mechanically, the Corvette was shaping up to be a great car: roomy, well balanced, and smooth. And the outward look of the car was changing too.

A TRIUMPH OF STYLING

The first thing people were going to notice about the 1963 Corvette wasn't a shorter wheelbase or an independent rear end. It was the sensational body which Bill Mitchell and his boys were fitting to the new chassis. Patterned (and eventually named) after the Sting Ray racer Mitchell and Shinoda unleashed in 1959, the '63 Corvette was one of the world's all-time great auto designs. Under its new boss, GM Styling was on a roll in the early '60s: The Sting Ray, Pontiac Grand Prix, and Buick Riviera all appeared within a single year. But the Sting Ray was the best of the best – Bill Mitchell's crowning achievement.

The shape had evolved over many years. GM Styling knew that its elements would sooner or later come together in a production Corvette, but no one could have known just how successful it would be. The Q-Corvette that began it all had an unfortunate rounded roof and fussy details around its wheels and nose. The production Sting Ray would be virtually perfect.

By the time the XP-720 mockup was put on display in October of 1959, the shape was more like

Mitchell's clean Sting Ray racer with the Q-Ship's roof grafted on. The car was originally seen as a coupe only, as the proposed 1958 replacement had been, but that idea was fortunately scotched by GM management.

Though the roof treatment was soon improved considerably, one feature of that first clay that did make production was a thick divider down the rear window. The divider incorporated a windsplit that ran from the windshield header to the lip of the ducktail, and Bill Mitchell absolutely loved it.

EVEN THOUGH *it was entirely new under the skin, the 1963's skin alone would have been enough for many buyers.*

Duntov and Mitchell were destined to go around and around over the so-called "split window" coupe. The engineer felt buyers had a right to see out of the back of their cars; the designer felt the bar was integral to the overall design. In an oft-repeated quote, Mitchell told Duntov "If you take that off, you might as well forget the whole thing."

In the end, both men won. The window split went into production but was summarily removed in 1964. These days split-window coupes are fairly rare – owners often took a hacksaw and removed the bar themselves.

Also contributing to the car's sleek design was its lack of exposed headlights. Hidden headlights were nothing new at the time – in fact quite the opposite: they were positively prehistoric, not having been seen since the 1942 De Soto. A number of proposals were put forward before the final rotating-nose design was settled on. Mitchell's designers tried flaps, bugeyes, and all sorts of other tricks, but the rotation idea remained far and away the best.

Making it work was another matter. Five different mechanical treatments were explored, and none was completely satisfactory. The method finally chosen used two modified electric window motors and made the car's nose a little wider than Styling had wanted. It was the best idea of the lot, but it still had problems; one of which was the manual override knobs hidden deep within the pointed nose. When the electric system failed, owners found that fiddling with the override knobs was only slightly worse than driving with no lights at all.

THE LONG-LIVED STINGRAY

Two years after the introduction of the '63 Sting Ray, and long before the public had tired of its unique styling, GM wanted a theme up and rolling for an entirely new Corvette for '67.

F1 WITH FENDERS

Well, not *entirely* new. Unlike the redesign in 1963, when Mitchell and Duntov had to simultaneously create and coordinate a whole new car, the '67 redesign seemed likely to affect only the Corvette's body. Much as Chevy had done to the Corvette in 1958, a new skin would give the Sting Ray the illusion of newness while relying on its time-proven platform for performance.

There *was* some talk of a mid- or rear-engined Corvette for '67, fueled particularly by the ascension of Pete Estes to the post of Chevrolet general manager in 1965. Engineers who'd been shot down previously hoped their new boss would be more receptive to this sort of pet project. But Bill Mitchell's faith was in a Sting Ray-based replacement, and that was the contingency he really planned for.

Suspecting he'd be working with the same platform as before, Mitchell's biggest problem was that his previous Corvette had been so successful. The worst thing a designer can do is propose a new model that's less attractive than the car it replaces, and it would take considerable effort to improve upon the 1963 Sting Ray.

Mitchell set down what he wanted from Larry Shinoda and his men. "Give me a Formula One car ... with fenders," he told them. Shinoda, and his assistant John Schinella, drew up some baseline sketches of sleek bodies with bulging, pontoon fenders. Mitchell liked their beginnings and started hammering away at the theme.

Under Mitchell's guidance and Shinoda's pen, the fenders became fluid with the body. They still stood out as the design's main theme, however; the first thing that caught the eye.

Taken into final sketches, Shinoda's high-fendered car was an exciting shape to say the least. At the front, a low, flat hood with finned air extractors rode between two peaked fenders. The nose itself had a prominent vee like the XP-755 Shark showcar. At the rear, a high deck and a long, tapered tail created tension and a crouching stance. Best of all, it was a completely new shape.

CORVETTE – *and all other makers of performance-orientated machines – were heading for a power output roller coaster over the next 20 years, with the mid-1970s as the low point, as emissions controls tightened and the oil crisis bit.*

Shinoda's drawings would become the Mako Shark II showcar. It would be as much a model for the late-'60s Corvette redesign as the original Sting Ray racer had been for the '63.

The Mako Shark II made its debut in April, 1965 at the New York Auto Show. Loaded with gadgets and legitimate looks at the future, it was an instant success with the crowds. Many in the enthusiast press, however, used it to engage in the popular new sport of Detroit bashing.

The Mako Shark II featured a removable targa roof, elaborately finned sidepipes (John Schinella put his body and soul into those), a 396 Mark IV engine, pop-up doors for the rear warning lights, and dozens of similar touches. There was no end to the details, both big and small, crammed into the Mako Shark II.

Many of them would eventually see production. The vacuum-powered panel which hid the windshield wipers was pretty whiz-bang stuff in '65, but it actually made production in '68. The Mako's clam-

LEFT Mitchell wanted "A Formula One car . . . with fenders." Shinoda and Schinella obliged him with the Mako Shark II of 1965.

shell hood saw the light of day on the 1984 Corvette. Body-colored nose and tail sections were installed on production Corvettes in 1973 and 1974, respectively, and the digital instruments which graced the Mako interior predated the production Corvette's LCD gauges by 19 years.

Two Mako Shark IIs would eventually be built, the 396-equipped, non-running New York Auto Show car, and a 427-powered driver. Distinguished primarily from the display car by its lack of elaborate sidepipes, the runner saw duty in Europe as a showcar and in America as Mitchell's personal machine.

The Mako Shark II had to be considerably tamed down before a production car could come out of it. When the time came to turn the Mako into a Corvette, Chevrolet engineers had to dictate many changes simply to make it producible. The hoodline had to be raised significantly to clear the car's mechanicals. Some form of bumper had to be applied to the nose. The Mako's quartz-iodide headlights

IT'S NOT *hard to see the family resemblance between Mako Shark II showcar (left) and a production '68 (below).*

had to be replaced with four retractable Sealed Beams.

The tail had to be most radically altered. The themes that held it together – a low roof, louvered rear window, and long, high ducktail with retractable spoiler – were unsuited to production. A talented designer named Alan Young put long hours into an all-new tail, and his skills show in the result. If anything, the rear clip of the proposed production model was cleaner and more integrated with the overall design than the Mako's original had been.

LATE RUNNER

Corvette trivia fans will have noticed by now that the new body was supposed to come out in 1967. But Corvettes didn't actually change over until 1968 – Engineering simply wouldn't let it happen. Zora Arkus-Duntov accepted the fact that styling played a big role in the Corvette's success, but he felt that the proposed '67 simply sacrificed too much function to achieve its good form.

"The car was not fit to drive on the street," he later said, citing that the front fenders were so high as to block forward vision. The deck design left the driver blind in back as well, and Duntov found the entire experience understandably disconcerting. After Duntov put his foot down, Larry Shinoda had

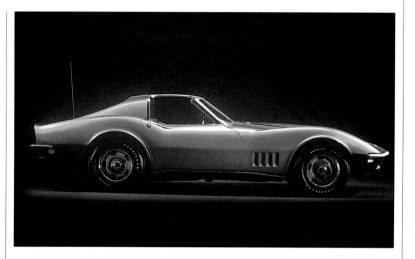

to do some skillful reworking of the shape before it was turned over to Hank Haga and Dave Holls' production studio. Finally, by the time everyone was pleased with the car, it was too late to be introduced as a 1967 model.

An all-new interior came along for the ride, and here again Duntov had reservations. The ancillary gauges had been moved from directly ahead of the steering wheel to a central console beneath eye level. This very clean interior theme would be in production through the 1982 model, however, and few people besides the perfectionist Duntov found fault with it.

Carried over for '68 were five engine choices: the 327/300, 327/350, and 427s with 390, 400, or 435 bhp. Actually, there were three 435-horse engines: the standard L71, the hotted-up L89, and the competition-spec L88. Also carried over was the Sting Ray's ladder frame, unchanged save for details of body and suspension mounting. A new Turbo Hydramatic transmission came on line to replace the Powerglide, and three 4-speed manuals – standard, close-ratio, and close-ratio heavy-duty – were offered as well.

Suspension changes had to be made to accommodate the new things happening on the surface. The 1968 body was about 100 pounds heavier than before, with most of the new weight right up front where the Corvette didn't need it.

Wider 7-inch wheels were fitted, and the suspension was tweaked to take advantage of their extra grip. But while the new setup improved handling, the Corvette's personality had been shifting from that of a canyon-carver to a straight-line, high-speed cruiser. Rather than appreciating the improved handling, many of the Corvette's new breed of buyers found fault with the stiffer, noisier ride that came with it.

But what really troubled the '68 was a simple lack of quality control. The big-block engine overheated magnificently, often destroying its optional aluminum heads in the process. Rain leaked into the cockpit. Doors and latches failed to work as intended. It was, for Chevrolet and Corvette, a very bleak period in what should have been a great year.

ZORA RETURNS

It didn't take Chevrolet long to realize the error of trying to integrate a machine as special as the Corvette into their mainstream engineering program. Nor did it take newly reappointed Corvette program boss Duntov – heads had rolled and a healthy Zora was called home to set things right – long to straighten the Corvette out. In the meantime, however, valuable prestige and customer loyalty had been lost.

To the public at large, fortunately, the Corvette's new body was a knockout. Despite the rough spots and poor reviews of the '68, a record-breaking 28,566 units were built. And quality woes or not, the car's performance was unquestionable – it surpassed the cornering power of the previous model and

Less debatable than the wisdom of the gauge layout was the fact that the new Corvette had much less interior space than the previous model, despite being seven inches longer overall. Mitchell's waspwaisted design gave up the interior gains of 1963 and then some. Shoulder room was tight, and luggage space shrunk significantly.

Zora Arkus-Duntov became quite sick during the final stages of development for the '68, and he disappeared from the scene for months. During the same period, a restructuring – a shakeup, if you like – occurred within the chain of command at Chevrolet and, when Zora returned, his role in the Corvette program had been slashed. He was no longer at the head but merely a special consultant. He had no real power. The Corvette became the responsibility of the same group that engineered Chevrolet's other products, and the '68 would suffer for it. Despite its year-long final gestation, it arrived truly under-engineered.

accelerated like gangbusters. An L88-equipped '68 with 4.11 Positraction would jump from 0–60 in less than five seconds flat, faster than anything a Corvette owner was likely to encounter.

Because of the bad reputation '68s gained early on, until quite recently they were something of a collector's bargain buy. Prices were reasonable since many buyers preferred the old-style '67 or the more refined '69. The troubles of the '68, however, were more of the annoying-but-easily-fixed variety rather than any sort of fatal flaws. A little work at home could bring them up to par with the best Corvettes of the '60s. Collectors have wised up since then, and a '68 Corvette – particularly a big-block convertible – will cost a packet now.

The '68 will have special meaning to at least one Corvette fan forever: his father's Le Mans Blue '68 convertible, with a close-ratio 4-speed and 427, was the first Corvette this author was lucky enough to drive.

When the 1969 model year rolled around, Zora Arkus-Duntov was ready. To make the car's interior more pleasant, Duntov stiffened the frame to reduce shakes and rattles. He added extra shoulder room through reshaped door panels. A smaller steering wheel gave the driver an increased sense of spaciousness and made entry and exit easier, and a new tilt option helped further still.

Overheating of the big-block engine was dramatically reduced. Zora used the plan he'd intended for

16

remaining big-block. The LS-5 wasn't offered in California, a victim of that state's much tighter emissions regulations.

By the way, there was one more change that made 1972 an important year in Corvette history: After 35 years, GM Styling changed its name. It's been known since May of '72 as GM Design Staff.

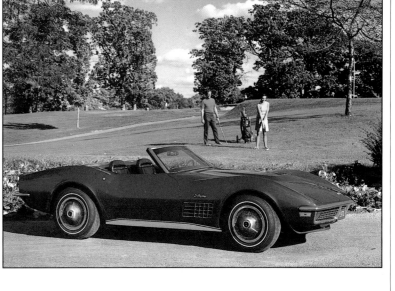

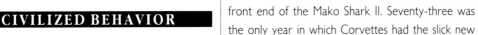
CIVILIZED BEHAVIOR

Nineteen seventy-three saw the first major changes to the Corvette body since 1970. Most noticeable was its new nose, a flexible, body-colored snout designed to meet the government's new regulations on impact resistance. One of these regs called for cars to withstand a 5 mph head-on collision without visible bumper or lighting damage. By passing impact energy through the rubber skin to two large deformable bolts, the Corvette met this goal handily. Ironically enough, the government-mandated nose also looked fantastic, harking back to the body-color

front end of the Mako Shark II. Seventy-three was the only year in which Corvettes had the slick new nose and the brutish old-style rear spoiler. It's earned a special collectability for the combination.

It was a year of refinement for the Corvette. Its body was attached to rubber bushings rather than the solid mounts used before, which resulted in fewer rattles and made the car seem tighter.

Speaking of rubber, a new type appeared on the car's wheels in 1973. Radial tires became standard, replacing the bias-plies of years past. While the radials lowered overall cornering grip, they were considerably quieter and smoother over the road. They also

ABOVE LEFT AND ABOVE RIGHT *1972, a year of change, was the last for chrome front bumpers and the first of net power ratings.*

BELOW LEFT *1973's federally mandated front bumper looked great, but the aluminum wheels were put off until 1976.*

improved the Corvette's wet-road behavior dramatically, an area of complaint from many owners. Heavier mats, undercoating, and insulation combined with the radials and rubber body mounts to make the '73 quieter and more civilized than any previous Corvette.

The 1970–1972 eggcrate side vents were replaced by functional single-scoop air extractors, and aluminum wheels were offered for the first time with the new bodystyle. Unfortunately, manufacturing problems kept the lightweight wheels from ever appearing on a showroom-bound car. The few '73s that got them were early publicity cars, or private cars retrofitted from supplies already shipped to dealers' parts departments.

Not surprisingly, power dropped once again as the grip of emissions laws tightened ever further. The base L48 engine made 190 net bhp, the L82

TOP RIGHT Pop-off T-roof panels, a nice compromise between coupe and convertible, were a Corvette mainstay for 14 years.

BELOW It wasn't all regs and fuel costs in '73: Chevy's 4-rotor experimental was often touted as the Corvette of the future.

BOTTOM The combination of old tail, new nose, and "sugar scoop" side vents made for an attractive and unique 1973 model.

small-block 250 bhp, and the LS4 454 came in at 275 net horses. Even with the base engine, however, Corvettes could still leap from 0–60 in less than seven seconds.

While the tire-smokers of the late '60s lamented the demise of their earthshaking engines, other buyers were finding out that they liked this new type of Corvette. It was quiet, agreeable, smooth, and handled like a dream. Though still plenty fast, it had cast off the rough edges, rattles, high-temperatures (both inside and out), and excessive thirst of a few years earlier.

Corvettes moved once again from the drag racer's market toward the quieter, more affluent buyers it was originally intended for. Increased sales of power steering, brakes, and automatic transmissions underscored the fact that once again buyers knew what the Corvette was all about. Women, too, were quickly becoming a large portion of the Corvette's market, something that would have surprised Harley Earl and Ed Cole in the early 1950s.

The bottom line was that they *sold*. By 1974, Corvette sales were beyond those of all but the

artificially lengthened 1969 model year. Seventy-four saw the completion of the change to body-colored, impact-absorbing bumpers. A rounded rear end – split vertically for this year only – appeared, and was at first rather controversial. Many people favored the more masculine tail of the earlier cars, but the new look was wholly in keeping with the Corvette's modern image.

It would be the last year of leaded fuel; catalytic converters came on line in 1975. Not coincidentally, 1974 was also the last year for the big-block engine. The 454 was by then emasculated to just 275 net bhp – a mere 30 horses more the '74 L82 small-block – and its acceleration was only marginally better than its lighter brother's. The big-block's cost in weight, handling, and mileage was too high for most buyers to bear. Fewer than 10% of the 37,502 Corvettes built that year had Mark IV power.

The last straw for the big-block was its failure to pass the government's tighter emissions tests for 1975. Time and money could have brought the engine into compliance, but Chevrolet correctly reasoned that in the midst of America's fuel crisis it was better to let the big-block die with dignity.

CORVETTE'S SWITCH *to impact-absorbing bumpers was completed in 1974. The vertical split in the rear bumper disappeared the following year.*

OIL CRISIS REFINEMENT

1975 brought a new type of Corvette to America. No, it looked just like the '74, except for some minor trim changes. But it was built for a world of costly fuel and increased safety concerns – its personality was that of a quick, responsible machine, rather than the rowdy hooligan it had been in recent memory. The heady days of cheap gas and a disorganized safety lobby were over. The Corvette was changing for the times. Output dropped again, this time to just 165 bhp for the L48, 205 bhp for the L84. Even considering that these were net figures, it

RIGHT *Trading brute strength for comfort, safety, and sophistication in 1975, sales climbed once more.*

BELOW *Reynolds Aluminium teamed with GM to build a lightweight version of the mid-engined XP-895. The girl was not included as standard.*

was the lowest output 2-engine lineup since 1955. It would be, in fact, the very lowest to which the Corvette's power levels would sink. By 1976, Detroit had gotten a grip on the realities of modern motoring and horsepower began to slowly rise back up.

Despite all this, the 1975 Corvette had plenty to recommend it. The interior had been upgraded constantly since '68, to the point that it was extraordinarily quiet and comfortable. The car felt light and willing, thanks to well calibrated power accessories, and it got respectable fuel mileage with or without the new 2.73 rear axle option.

An explosion-proof rubber bladder was hidden inside the fuel tank which made a fuel fire almost impossible. Front and rear bumper designs were changed to be even sturdier. Where the 1973 and 1974 used rubber over metal supports and deformable bolts, the 1975 had an all-new impact system of hydraulic dampers. Rather than deforming anything, the bumpers just bounced back.

Both the Corvette's price and 0–60 times climbed. A reasonably optioned car now easily passed the $7000 mark, and 0–60s were back up to the high 7-second range. There was, of course, still nothing on the road that could touch the Corvette's combination of price and performance. But the figures weren't nearly as staggering as they'd been a few years before.

Another victim of the mid-'70s drive toward responsible motoring was the Corvette convertible. 1975 would be its last year – or so it was believed. The convertible revival of the '80s was completely

unexpected during the fuel- and safety-conscious days of 1975. Convertibles seemed profligate and frivolous to the public, and sales suffered accordingly. By 1975 just 12% of the near-record 38,465 Corvettes produced had open tops. At those figures, it wasn't worth Chevrolet's effort and expense to keep producing convertibles. The 1974 and 1975 convertible were some of the best-looking Corvettes of all time, but they were expected to be the end of the ragtop line.

One more change made 1975 a significant year for Corvette. On January 1, 1975 Zora Arkus-Duntov officially retired from Chevrolet. The man who'd coaxed, guided, and nurtured the Corvette – and the GM brass who controlled its fate – for more than 20 years, was going into retirement.

David R. McLellan took his place. McLellan's boyish looks betrayed little of his extensive experience in automotive engineering, testing, and design. Zora's departure left a fantastic void, and many people doubted that anyone so youthful in appearance and outlook could take his place. Dave McLellan would prove them wrong.

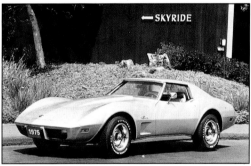

→ SKYRIDE

DAVID McLELLAN: SILVER ANNIVERSARY

One of the first things buyers noticed about the 1976 car – the first "McLellan" Corvette – was that horsepower rates had climbed again. It as an admittedly small jump: five bhp for the L82, giving it a total of 210 horsepower, but at least it was a ray of hope for the future.

The aluminum wheels that were cancelled in '73 finally came on line in '76, giving the car a much-appreciated modern touch. A snappier torque converter helped 0–60 times drop below seven seconds

ABOVE AND LEFT *1975 marked a turning point for Corvette. In a relatively short time it had come to terms with modern demands.*

EVER-INCREASING *sophistication was matched by a resurgence in power levels in McLellan's first Corvette, the 1976.*

again, and Corvette sales soared to more than 46,500 units. The next year, 1977, saw a minor interior re-design – though the gauges remained in the same layout, a new central console gave the interior a fresher, high-tech appearance.

The 1977 model also set new standards for fast, safe, and rewarding handling. Its overall grip was good, but its transition and response were without equal. ROAD & TRACK set a new slalom speed

record for their magazine with a 1977 L82, besting the runner-up 911 Turbo Carrera by almost one mph. Luxurious leather seats became standard equipment that same year, as did power brakes and steering, but the base price climbed by more than $1000 to nearly $8700. Despite this unprecedented jump, production ran just shy of the magic 50,000 mark.

But it was the 1978 model that would really show McLellan's stuff. 1978 marked the 25th anniversary of the Corvette, and everyone knew that a major celebration was called for. Big plans were in the works to commemorate this milestone for Chevy's favorite son.

The most obvious addition to the now-10-year-old Corvette body was a sleek glass fastback, im-proving both aerodynamics and interior room con-siderably. The bubbleback added space for T-tops, grocery bags, luggage, or a few fetally-curled friends on the daily lunch run. Originally planned as a true hatchback with opening glass, a fixed rear window appeared on the production car. As with the '63–'68 coupes, fixed glass presented few real problems for the owners. When they wanted something from the back, they just reached, however ingloriously, over the seats.

McLellan and Chevrolet also squeezed a little more power from the venerable 350 small-block, five extra horses for the L48 and 10 more for the L82. Larger exhaust tracts did the trick, and the L82 received a new intake system as well. Unfortunately, no L82s went on sale that year in emissions-strict California.

Bringing the L82 up to 220 honest bhp meant that 0–60 times dropped once again to the mid-6-second range. Large, sticky Goodyear radials (255/70R-15), brought the Corvette's lateral acceleration to within a breath of the magic .80g mark at the same time.

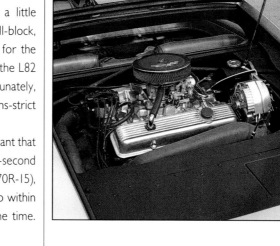

While not posting quite the same slalom speeds as the 1977, the '78 Corvette cut an impressive figure over twisty roads.

The slower slalom times were probably the result of a shift in front/rear weight distribution from 49/51 to 46/54. This slightly upset overall balance, but the added rear traction was good news on slick pavement; in short, the monster Goodyears made the Corvette easier to drive fast than ever before.

Left-foot driving was the favorite pastime of L82 owners, but a new instrument panel and interior made plain old cruising a delight for all. The tachometer and speedo were removed from their individual pods and placed together in a single recessed box ahead of the driver. New door panels, cleaner and better finished than before, were added, and visibility through the new rear glass was superb. Finally, a pull-out screen allowed owners to hide their belongings in the car's rear.

In addition to all these mechanical advances, two semi-cosmetic option packages made the 1978 model year a collector's dream. The Silver Anniversary model featured a sophisticated two-tone paint scheme of light silver above dark silver; its interior

ABOVE LEFT *Kelsey-Hayes aluminum wheels appeared for good in 1976. Earlier versions were cancelled due to manufacturing woes.*

TOP AND ABOVE *When the fuel crunch put a Kaibosh on GM's rotary program the 4-rotor got a 400-inch V-8 and new name: Aerovette.*

LEFT *Fully aware of whose shoes he had to fill, David R. McLellan took over from Zora Arkus-Duntov on January 1, 1975.*

was treated to silver carpets, and mandatory aluminum wheels and sport mirrors came along for the
ride. Silver Anniversary cars sold like mad, despite
their $780 surcharge – $400 for paint, $340 for
wheels, and $40 for mirrors.

The Silver Anniversary package wasn't cheap. Its
price was chickenfeed, however, compared to the
Limited Edition Corvette option – the so-called Pace
Car. As they had with the 1969 Camaro, Chevrolet
arranged to have a new Corvette pace the field for

the 1978 Indianapolis 500. A special commemorative
edition was a must.

With base Corvettes selling for an already-hefty
$9352, the Pace Car's $13,653 pricetag was a
whopper. For that money, though, buyers got a
bushel-basket of regular and special options thrown
up. Most noticeable were the black and silver two-
tone paint and unique spoilers. Also included were
high-back bucket seats, power windows and door
locks, air conditioning, tilt/telescope steering, aluminum

ABOVE *With optional FE7 gymkhana suspension, 1977 boasted stellar handling. Journalists found it exceptionally easy to drive fast.*

BELOW *The low, long Aerovette had drag numbers as good as its looks: .325 Cd; most cars were lucky to break .40.*

RIGHT *Perhaps out of respect for its elders, this 1978 shows great restraint in not smoking off its pristine 1953 rival.*

wheels, and much, much more. Chevrolet even included a set of owner-applied decals, reading *Official Pace Car*, for people who really wanted to stick out in traffic.

The company had originally planned to build just 1000 Pace Car replicas, but eventually made one for each dealer and change. In all, 6,502 Pace Cars were built, and uncounted '78s were converted to bogus Pace Car spec afterwards. Dealers were asking, and receiving, prices far above invoice for the black-and-silver specials, and a number of unscrupulous private owners wanted a share of the profits.

After such a big blowout, the 1979 models were understandably similar to the 1978s. Another five horses came to the L82, and 10 more were offered with the L48. Spoilers, basically the same as those on the '78 Pace Car, were also offered for $265. Installed, they decreased drag by about 15%.

MOVING UPMARKET

By 1980, the Corvette was undeniably showing its age. But it was definitely showing a timelessness as well. Still one of the best sports car bargains – one of

ABOVE *Designers originally conceived the aerodynamic 1978 backlight as an opening hatch; production models got fixed glass.*

LEFT *Two-tone Silver Anniversary option package made for one of the best-looking and most collectible Corvettes to date.*

the best sports cars, period – on the market, it continued to attract an ever-growing following.

But Chevrolet knew that the once-radical shape had become all too familiar to a world that had seen the Mazda RX-7, Porsche 928, Ferrari 308, and Datsun Z-Cars appear in the '70s. In response, McLellan's Corvette group was well on its way to designing an all-new machine for 1983. Until then, however, they were determined to keep the Corvette as current and competitive as it had always been.

Their answer to the newer competition came in the form of some truly modern upgrades. The 1980 Corvette was about 250 pounds trimmer than the 1979, through the use of lighter bumper assemblies, thinner door and windshield materials, a combined differential housing/crossmember made of aluminum, and an aluminum intake manifold for the L48. These and other measures improved acceleration, handling, and fuel economy.

Though still a young science in Detroit, a lot of thought was given to the car's aerodynamic drag. The Corvette's Cd (coefficient of drag) was dropped 12% below the already slippery Pace Car's figures with redesigned front and rear end caps.

Also arriving on the scene in the early '80s were CAFE (Corporate Average Fuel Economy) ratings, a

system by which the government dealt fines to cars and companies with poor gas mileage. GM swore that they wouldn't let a single car fall to a CAFE "gas-guzzler" tax, and a fuel-sipping 3.07:1 rear axle became mandatory for the Corvette.

California buyers felt the hand of the government in a different, even heavier way. Chevrolet declined to certify the 350-cid engine for California's new and highly restrictive emissions regulations. Instead, they outfitted Corvettes headed for that state with the 305 cid V-8, an engine already California-certified ("Californicated") for the Camaro. Fitted with tubular stainless steel headers the 305 still produced a respectable 180 bhp, but to some it seemed an ominous sign. Exactly 3221 305-equipped Corvettes were built, a considerably smaller percentage of production than California traditionally absorbed. It can only be assumed that a lot of people headed across state lines to purchase their new Corvette.

Despite their aggressive new looks and lightweight bodies, Corvette production was off by more than 20% for 1980. More than 53,800 1979s had been made: 1980 production settled in just above a less impressive 40,000.

1981 Corvettes carried an essentially unchanged exterior, but differences abounded elsewhere. The first thing people noticed was the L81, a new engine, and the removal of the long-standing L48 and L82. Much to the relief of the doom merchants, the California 305 was gone as well. In its place, though, was something perhaps even *more* ominous: a single, 50-state engine with 190 bhp. The 350-cid L81 eliminated the cost of producing three separate engines for the Corvette, but it put an end to higher output cars for those willing to pay the price.

Fortunately, the mandatory L81 was a fine engine. With magnesium rocker covers and stainless-steel

exhausts, it promised to make good on GM's promise of healthy power and mileage through technology. Computer Command Control, Chevrolet's name for their black-box electronic control module (ECM), handled the engine's emissions settings, timing, and intake mixture. The ECM adjusted these variables 10 times a second, according to inputs from sensors at the intake, exhaust, transmission, and elsewhere.

OPPOSITE PAGE AND ABOVE *By the end of the decade, Corvettes like this modified '78 were once again hunting on European soil.*

BELOW *The deep, aerodynamic chin of 1980-1982 models was functional as well as attractive. A matching deck spoiler graced the rear.*

ABOVE *1980s technology came on board in 1981 with computers, a fiberglass monoleaf rear spring, and stainless exhaust manifolds.*

Another high-tech feature of the '81 Corvette was its GRP (fiberglass) rear spring, which came on all cars with automatic transmissions and the standard suspension. At a mere eight pounds compared to the steel spring's 44 it would soon be available across the board.

By 1981, the base Corvette cost more than $16,250. This was still considerably less than anything in its performance league, but quite a bit more than the new breed of sports cars like RX-7 and 280ZX.

ABOVE *With a full 350 back under the hood, California Corvette drivers took to the hills again in 1981.*

Corvette's march upmarket was in many ways deliberate. Since Chevrolet had long been able to out-sell their production capacity with the car, prices and equipment standards had risen steadily.

Part of the increasing cost of Corvettes, however, was the result of outdated manufacturing equipment at the St. Louis assembly plant. St. Louis had been making the car in the same plant since 1954, and Chevrolet was ready to switch to a new, highly automated Corvette assembly facility in

Bowling Green, Kentucky. On June 1, 1981, Bowling Green took over production. St. Louis built cars simultaneously until August 1, then ceased Corvette production. Missouri's loss would be the Corvette lover's gain: Bowling Green's advanced facilities were, and are, ideally suited to the high-technology assembly required of today's Corvettes.

There were remarkably few teething woes with the new plant, and most buyers were unaware that such a major manufacturing change had taken place. Part of the easy transition can be attributed to GM's attempts to attract as many former St. Louis employees to Bowling Green as possible. Almost all of the line workers at Bowling Green had moved the 300 miles from St. Louis to take up their old jobs at the new factory.

Though they had to pay their own moving costs, the company helped with just about everything else. They offered assistance in finding housing and health care, provided social services, and opened large parts of the plant for community tours and meetings. As we'll see in the next chapter, Bowling Green became a model facility, both in working conditions and product quality.

LAST OF ITS KIND

It was no secret, even in the very early '80s, that an all-new Corvette was waiting in the wings. That 1982 would be the swan-song of the Mitchell/Shinoda bodystyle and the Cole/Duntov underpinnings was a well-known fact.

It was good news, to be sure; in the auto business, progress always is. But there were definitely those

1982 CORVETTES, all built in the new high-tech plant at Bowling Green, Kentucky, featured TBI Cross Fire Injection.

who would miss "the old girl," as the Corvette became known, and Chevy decided to make 1982 a fitting send-off for the platform that had served them so well for so long. Part of that send-off would be to give the car a healthy taste of the all-new model to come.

The year-old L81 gave way to the L83, a throttle-body-injected (TBI) 350 with 200 bhp. Its Cross Fire Injection system had nothing in common with the old Rochester constant-flow FI of 1957–1965.

Essentially, Cross Fire Injection used two electronic throttle bodies, one near each rocker cover, to squirt fuel directly into a single-plane aluminum intake manifold. From there the fuel/air mixture traveled through tuned intake runners to ports on the opposite side of the engine. The left-hand injector fed the right-hand cylinder bank and vice-versa; hence the name Cross Fire.

The ECM that made 10 decisions a second in 1981 was made capable of 80 adjustments a second with the TBI engine. Because of this new-found precision over timing and mixture, compression could be bumped from 8.2:1 to 9.0:1.

A new 4-speed automatic overdrive transmission became the only gearbox available, a high-tech job called the THM 700-R4. Having four gears, the top three with positive lockup, meant that 1st could be lower than before while 4th could be higher. Low and high gear ratios on the previous 3-speed auto-

DELICATE PAINT, *badging, and wheels set off the highly coveted Collector Edition.*

matic had been 2.52:1 and 1.00:1, respectively. On the 4-speed, they became 3.06:1 and 0.70:1.

The new powertrain was mandatory on all 1982s, but not all '82s were alike. At $22,538, the 1982 Collector Edition Corvette was the most expensive car Chevrolet had ever offered. It was also one of the most sophisticated and subtly attractive.

The Collector Edition's unique silver-grey metallic paint was set off by graduated gray decals on the hood and flanks. Delicately finished cloisonne medals graced the wheel centers and end caps. Aluminum wheels similar to those on the '63–'67 Corvette appeared, as did a luxurious leather and deep-pile carpet interior. Transparent T-top panels with a subtle bronze tint were unique to the car, and the Collector Edition was also the only Corvette of its generation to get a lift-up rear hatch.

All in all, the 1982 Corvette was widely appreciated as the last of a wonderful series of cars. It was the final expression of an inimitable character: a big, solid, fast, sports car that could be tame as a kitten in town but downright ferocious on the open road.

It was with great anticipation that the world looked forward to the next model – the first all-new Corvette in 20 years. But it was also with a bit of nostalgia and remorse. Since 1963, the Corvette had supplied the world with its own unique brand of fun and magic – no matter how good the next generation would be, they'd never build them the same way again.

ONLY THE COLLECTOR
Edition got an opening hatch in the old-style body. That and its unique detailing make it a rare find.

THE
CURRENT
GENERATION

Most people will tell you that there were no 1983 Corvettes. They're wrong. True, when the first customer cars were shipped out in February of '83, Chevy had already decided to register and sell them as 1984 models. They wanted to have the first '84s on the market, rather than the last '83s.

But the first 43 cars – 10 prototypes and 33 pilot vehicles – were, in fact, assembled with 1983 build plates and VINs (Vehicle Identification Numbers). Since none of these were ever sold to the public, they're often overlooked in Corvette lore. You can win a few bar bets with this one, though.

Production Corvettes #0002 through #0070 were built as test vehicles, though most of the later cars were eventually sold off. The serial number 0001 was reserved for the 71st Corvette built, which was donated to the National Council of Corvette Clubs' spina bifida charity raffle. The first customer-

1985 models had just one readily visible difference: subtle Tuned Port Injection badges on the beltline.

TPI *(Tuned Port Injection) appeared in '85, bringing 25 more horses and a more usable delivery curve to the venerable 350.*

plaints popped up. The top-of-the-line Z51 suspension was one trouble spot. It was, apparently, too much of what the magazines had asked for.

The base suspension and tires delivered more grip than most writers had ever encountered, yet the Z51 was stiffer and stickier still. Too much so, many felt. There was even an unsubstantiated rumor that went as far as saying the Z51 could crack the roof panel if the car went over a sharp bump.

Some writers also complained that the car was too heavy, being only about 250 pounds lighter than its predecessor. That its weight and performance compared admirably with the Porsche 928S, BMW 633, and Ferrari 308 was rarely mentioned. Other drivers, wanting a dramatic, heart-pounding confrontation with the new Corvette, were disappointed by the car's easy-going nature. It went *calmly* like a bat out of hell, without all the noise and chassis-jacking of the competition. Many drivers, apparently, didn't realize just how fast they were really going.

THE RAGTOP RETURNS

Much as with Corvettes past, the history of the car's current generation is one of subtle refinements for major results. In its first year it was good enough to be MOTOR TREND's Car of the Year. Annual upgrades ensured not only a constantly improved package but a yearly appearance as one of CAR & DRIVER's Ten Best Performers.

The first big changes came in '85, though you'd be hard-pressed to see them from the outside. Tuned Port Injection (TPI) came on line to replace the previous car's Cross Fire (TBI) system. With one injector at each intake port, rather than the TBI's two for the entire engine, port injection added 25 horsepower and 40 ft./lbs. of torque. ROAD & TRACK measured 0–60 times for the hopped-up 'Vette at 6.2 seconds and their quarter-mile sprint took just 8.2 seconds more. TPI also gave a whopping 11% boost in EPA-rated fuel mileage.

That same year, shock and spring rates were refined to smooth out the Z51's behavior on rough roads. Wider front tires – up an inch to a full 9.5 – improved overall handling despite the more civilized settings.

In 1986, Bosch ABS II anti-lock brakes were added to the package. Without getting into too much detail, the Bosch system would automatically

bought car was #0071, the 70th car off the line. Cochran & Celli, an Oakland, California, Chevy dealer, sold it to Mr. Bob Nagy.

The media's reaction to the car was, in a word, ecstatic, though they'd been expecting a new car since '72 and crying out for a mid-engined model. Those two facts should have made the new car, no matter how good, a disappointment to many. It wasn't.

"A Star is Born," said MOTOR TREND. "Fantastic," was the word from ROAD & TRACK. "America takes on all comers," quoth CAR & DRIVER. Let loose for early previews in pilot cars and engineering specials, the country's auto journalists waxed poetic over the new Corvette's looks, handling and performance.

As the year progressed, production models trickled into the magazines' stables and a few com-

LEFT *TPI also gave owners a whopping 11% increase in fuel economy and another 40 foot-pounds of torque.*

BELOW *This was the most common view of the 1985 Corvette. The car was more than a match for machines three times the price.*

adjust brake fluid pressure to prevent panic-stop lockups. Accelerating to 60 mph in about six seconds, by '86 the Corvette could decelerate back to zero in less than 130 feet! The only other car with that sort of braking was Ferrari's BB512 Boxer. Lacking ABS, however, it took an expert driver to get the Boxer's braking distances down that low.

Eighty-six also saw the return of the long-rumored Corvette convertible. Introduced in mid-year, the trim ragtop sported a folding roof and, once again, aluminum cylinder heads. The lightweight aluminum heads were finally here to stay: they became standard as soon as production got up to speed.

Because the Corvette was already a full targa, surprisingly little additional bracing was required for the convertible conversion. Basically, a hefty X-brace was added beneath the passenger compartment and the K-braces at the cowl were beefed up.

SINCE THE *super-stiff coupes were already full targas, convertibles needed very little extra structural bracing.*

Anyone familiar with the 1968–1975 Corvette droptop already knew how the current convertible top operates. A fiberglass panel at the rear of the passenger compartment hid the assembly in the down position. To put the top up, the driver opened the panel (electrically or with a manual override), attached the header rail to the windshield, put the panel back down, and pushed two guide pins into holes on the rear deck. Despite its simplicity, the padded top was remarkably snug when erected.

The 200-horse L83 of 1982 evolved – through cam and induction changes, roller lifters, compression-ratio jumps, and so on – into the 245 bhp L98 of 1988. With torque climbing to a lofty 330 ft./lbs., Chevy's official 0–60 time for the manually-shifted L98 dropped to 5.3 seconds.

That same year, Corvettes received new wheels, the first significant external change since '84. The Z51 package now offered 13-inch front discs (12-inchers were standard) and larger 17-inch wheels to clear the oversized rotors. The standard 16-inchers were redesigned in the bargain.

ABOVE *1988 brought optional 13-inch brake discs and 17-inch wheels to the race-bred Z51.*

RIGHT *Corvette seats, real leather and adjustable for everything short of blood types, were often hailed as the best in the business.*

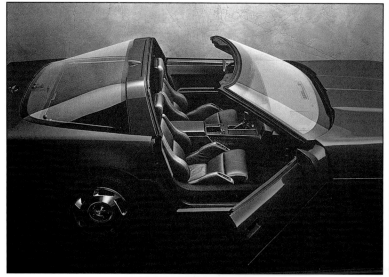

TOP RIGHT *A GTO body kit, developed for racing but sold through Chevy dealers, was considered a legitimate Corvette option.*

ABOVE RIGHT AND RIGHT *White body-color wheels and a stand-out black roof pillar distinguished 1988 35th Anniversary model.*

AFTERMARKET WHEELS *(above) were a favorite addition, but production items (center right) inspired many imitators.*

RIGHT *Headlights rotated on an axis perpendicular to the driveline. Plenty of headaches went into getting them right.*

OPPOSITE *The fast and elusive Western Mountain Corvette, seen here in its natural habitat, is far from extinction.*

CALLAWAY

In October of 1986, auto enthusiasts received official confirmation of a rumor they'd long been hoping was true. Their favorite magazines let them know that Chevrolet, in a murkily defined relationship with Callaway Engineering of Old Lyme, Connecticut, would offer a 345-horse twin-turbo Corvette for sale to the public.

Chevy did their best to downplay their affiliation with Callaway, but there was little doubt that the companies were in full cahoots. Chevy even assigned the Callaway its own option number: RPO B2K made the twin-turbo an official Chevrolet, covered by the same type of warranties and dealer network that any other of their products enjoyed.

The $51,000 Callaway was the fastest car this side of the Ferrari Testarossa and GTO, both of which cost well over $110,000. It turned quarter miles in 13 seconds flat, 0–60s in about 4.5 seconds, and topped out just shy of 180 mph. More than one Corvette

ABOVE *Though missing the usual roof-pillar badging, the airy wheels and high top end of this Corvette spelled Callaway.*

BELOW *Fair warning to Ferrari and Porsche drivers, the LT5 emblem stood for big numbers: 4 cams, 385 bhp, 180+ mph.*

B2K headed off to the *Autobahn* to settle some old scores. By the time Callaway arrived, Chevy had been playing with twin-turbo 'Vettes for quite a while. At first these were V-6-powered experimentals, built toward the day when a V-6 Corvette might be necessary to meet CAFE quotas. Later, twin-turbo V-8s were built just to see how fast a Corvette could really go.

"Thumper," one of those force-fed V-8s, was seeing nearly 200 mph by the time the Callaway was born. Chevrolet could certainly have built a car like the Callaway on its own – were GM of a mind to allow it. But Reeves Callaway, the acknowledged leader in aftermarket turbos, was an easy way around management's worries.

Officially, Chevrolet never sold Callaways. They sold turbo-ready B2Ks to which Callaway added all the necessary hardware, and it was up to the dealer to purchase the car from there. GM didn't release material or advertising on the twin-turbos, and never mentioned them as products. They did, however, provide Callaway with engineering support, an RPO and warranty as mentioned, and specially-prepared B2K blocks.

ZR1: AMERICAN SUPERCAR

But the Callaway's status as the ultimate American car changed with the arrival of the next – and this time fully GM-blessed – super Corvette. Listen to this: 385 bhp, 180+ mph, six forward speeds, 30 mpg, $49,000, 4 cams, 32 valves, and 16 individual intake runners. Want one?

Well, all you had to do was go down to your local Chevy dealer and order up a Corvette with RPO ZR1. You'd find yourself in possession of the fastest, most advanced Corvette ever.

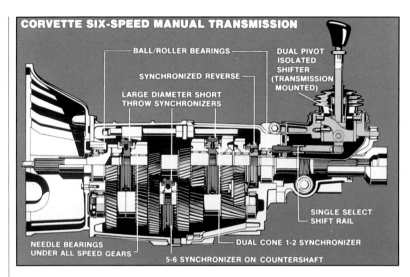

CORVETTE SIX-SPEED MANUAL TRANSMISSION

BALL/ROLLER BEARINGS

DUAL PIVOT ISOLATED SHIFTER (TRANSMISSION MOUNTED)

SYNCHRONIZED REVERSE

LARGE DIAMETER SHORT THROW SYNCHRONIZERS

SINGLE SELECT SHIFT RAIL

NEEDLE BEARINGS UNDER ALL SPEED GEARS

5-6 SYNCHRONIZER ON COUNTERSHAFT

DUAL CONE 1-2 SYNCHRONIZER

TOP LEFT *The six-speed ZF gearbox, introduced in 1989, marked a new high point in production car transmission technology.*

TOP RIGHT *Only subtle differences on the outside – rounded end cap, squared taillights, wider rear body – graced the 1989 ZR1.*

ABOVE *Giant rear tires were needed to get all that LT5 power to the ground, and a widened rear body appeared in turn to cover them.*

LEFT *Many journalists called the ZR1 the Heart Attack, not Heartbeat, of America.*

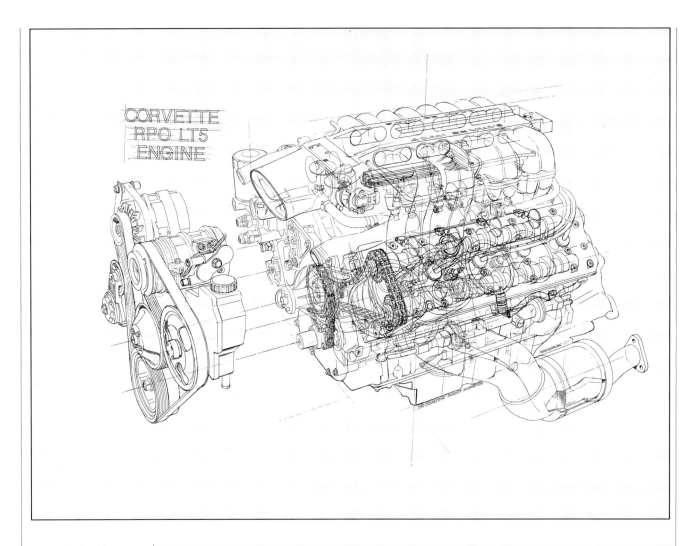

CORVETTE
RPO LT5
ENGINE

ABOVE *Ordered by Chevrolet, designed by Lotus, and built by Mercury Marine: a lot goes on inside the powerhouse LT5.*

RIGHT *Promised from the start of convertible production in '86, a sharp-looking hardtop finally appeared in '89.*

The ZRI's heart was the LT5 engine, an all-aluminum, normally aspirated quad-cam developed by Lotus, GM's newly acquired engineering division. What began as a program to put 4-valve heads on the L98 evolved into an all-new, super-high-tech engine. The LT5 shared just one component, the rear main bearing seal, with the regular 350 Chevy.

Chevrolet set down seemingly impossible targets for the 32-valve engine. It was to have more power than the big-blocks of days gone by, fit into the already snug Corvette engine bay without a hood scoop, and be more docile than the babydoll L98. And while you're at it, GM told Lotus, give it better mileage than the L98, too.

Amazingly, the LT5 fulfilled all those goals. It was actually two engines in one – two distinctly different intake and valve packages were included in the single powerplant. Each cylinder had two intake and two exhausts valves, two port injectors, and two tuned intake runners. The primaries were for regular driving – the secondary pieces came into play for all-out performance.

The primary intake system was fed by a single .87-inch butterfly. This meted out air to the eight primary intake runners, which led to valves operated

TOP *Though the padded soft top did an excellent job, dealers sold hardtops individually to retrofit 1986 and later convertibles.*

There are very few differences in the skins of models produced between 1984 and 1989 (shown here). The convertible was first introduced in mid-1986.

by a set of mildly-ground lobes on the overhead camshaft.

This small-induction, low-overlap formula was good for low-end torque, driveability, and fuel efficiency. Running on just this primary circuit, the LT5 gave about the same performance as the L98.

Get into the gas, though, and the secondary intake system kicked in: two 2.32-inch throttle plates slapped open and oxygen poured into the remaining eight intake runners. Port injectors dumped fuel directly upstream of intake valves bumped by a second set of lobes, these ones with a radical, high-overlap grind. It was the secondary system that supplied the LT5's prodigious top-end power.

The ZR1 put that power to the ground through massive 315/35ZR-17 tires, the largest then offered in America. In plain talk, the tires were 315mm (12.4 inches) wide, mounted on 17-inch wheels, and rated for sustained speeds over 180 mph. The ZR1 carried all-new rear bodywork to cover the giant rubber, though only the square lamps in a slightly more rounded tail cap were an obvious tip-off to what lurked under the hood.

In addition, the ZR1 had a unique "valet" switch –

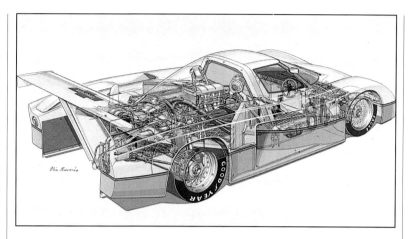

a key-controlled lockout for the heavy-duty butterflies and injectors. This allowed the ZR1 to be driven by valets, kids, mothers-in-law, and anyone else the regular driver didn't think was quite ready for 385 horses.

Despite all these things – and variable-damping shocks, a 6-speed ZF transmission it shared with all manual '89s, and more – the ZR1 went on sale for a couple of thousand dollars less than the B2K Callaway. Buyers could, in theory anyway, get change back from their $50,000.

AMA RACING BANS *having faded like a bad memory, Corvette GTP won twice in 1986 and set an IMSA record, capturing seven pole positions.*

ABOVE *1988 SCCA Trans-Am; winners at Mosport.*

RIGHT *1988 GTP.*

BELOW *Invincible in Showroom Stock, SCCA set Corvettes up in their own one-car series called Corvette Challenge.*

And oh yes, one more thing: with its super-wide rear tires, the ZR1 was not only the fastest Corvette to date, it was the best handling as well. It could pull 1.2g through corners – more than most racing cars.

Racing cars, by the way, seem once again to hold the future of the Corvette. After finally renouncing their compliance with the AMA racing ban, factory-assisted Corvettes and Corvette-based competition cars are once again winning races around the world. Led by names like Childress, Brassfield, Protofab, and Peerless, silhouette and prototype Corvettes are the terror of American road racing. There are IMSA GTO and GTP Corvettes, SCCA Trans-Am entries, drag racers, and more.